NARROW GAUG
MINIATURE RAI
FROM OLD PICTURE POSTCARDS

by Andrew Neale

MINIATURE RAILWAY, MARINE LAKE, RHYL   W 2055

Plateway Press, 13 Church Road, Croydon, Surrey, CR0 1SG.

ISBN 0 9511108 0 2

British Library Cataloguing in Publication Data

Neale, Andrew
Narrow gauge and miniature railways from old picture
postcards.

1. Postal cards – Great Britain
2. Railroads, Narrow gauge – Great Britain – Pictorial works
1. Title
769'. 49385520941   NE 1878. R34
ISBN 0-951110-80-2

Printed in Great Britain by Wayzgoose Ltd, Boston Road, Sleaford, Lincs.

Front cover illustration: Epitome of the English narrow gauge railway was the Lynton and
Barnstaple. LPC's colour tinted card shows EXE, second of the three original Manning
Wardle 2-6-2T's. posed on the locomotive shed road at Lynton station about 1905.

Back cover illustration: The set of six LPC colour tinted cards of the Ravenglass and
Eskdale Railway, published in December 1915 are amongst the earliest of this railway. The
line's first locomotive, Bassett-Lowke 4-4-2 SANSPAREIL poses at Muncaster Mill with a
train of Heywood stock.
(Both pictures courtesy Real Photographs Co.)

Title page illustration: A sepia toned commercial postcard, published by Valentine's of
Dundee, depicting one of the Barnes Atlantic 4-4-2's on the 15" gauge Rhyl Miniature
Railway, in the mid 1950's.
(Courtesy Valentine's of Dundee Ltd.)

INTRODUCTION – The Narrow Gauge Railway

The narrow gauge railway is both father to, and child of, the Industrial Revolution. The earliest recorded uses of narrow gauge railways were in the metal mines of Central Europe in the late 15th Century using primitive wooden rails and wagons. Not until the early 17th Century were the first 'tramroads' built, at first with wooden rails and later with plate or edge rails of iron. Most lines were used to convey coal from mine shafts to navigable waterways or a nearby ironworks. Examples were to be found in Britain in the 18th and early 19th Century, particularly in the North East, South Wales and the Coalbrookdale area of Shropshire.

An early tinted postcard illustrating typical use of narrow gauge railways within a colliery complex –in this case the 2'0" gauge system at Ashington Colliery in Northumberland.

Eventually the tramroads evolved into early locomotive worked railways, via Trevithick's brief experiment with a locomotive on the Pen-y-Darren tramroad in 1804, and led to the eventual adoption of 4'8½" gauge (just one of the many competing gauges in use up to 1800) as the 'standard' gauge for Britain's main line railways.

Following a separate but parallel line of development, the origins of today's narrow gauge railways are in North Wales, where in 1800 output at slate quarries such as Penrhyn and Dinorwic was limited to what could be carried by pack horses. A 2'0" gauge tramroad from Penrhyn quarry to the coast (opened in 1801) was the first successful application of narrow gauge technology on a large scale. Other lines followed – the Padarn Railway in 1824, Nantlle in 1828, and the Festiniog in 1836. The early slate railways closed with the decline of their staple traffic but the Festiniog and Talyllyn (1865) which had diversified into passenger traffic, survived into the present era.

Outside North Wales, exploitation of raw materials was also the catalyst. The 2'4½" gauge Glyn Valley Tramway (1873) connected the Shropshire Union Canal with slate and granite workings at Pandy. The Ravenglass and Eskdale (3'0" gauge) was opened in 1875 to exploit iron ore workings, and the 2'3" gauge Campbeltown and Macrihanish Railway evolved from a local colliery railway (1877). These and other similar lines soon began to supplement their staple traffic with local passenger traffic and those railways in attractive areas found 'holiday' traffic a useful if fickle bonus.

The major phase of narrow gauge railway development was the promotion of purely 'common carrier' railways including the 3'0" gauge Southwold (1879) and Rye and Camber (1895), Lynton & Barnstaple (1'11½" gauge, 1898), Welshpool & Llanfair (2'6" gauge, 1903) and Leek & Manifold (1904). These railways were not tied to any staple traffic, and had to compete vigorously for every scrap of business. Thus evolved the classic rural railway, serving nowhere of any real importance, using quaint and increasingly antiquated locomotives and rolling stock, with an overworked staff struggling against arrears of maintenance to run the advertised service.

An inherent weakness of all narrow gauge railways was the need to tranship freight from narrow to standard gauge wagons, a time-consuming, costly process. Only the Leek and Manifold tackled the problem properly, using transporter wagons to carry standard gauge wagons, though this would have been impossible on many other narrow gauge lines, with their limited clearances under bridges and in tunnels and cuttings.

The growth of road haulage and rural bus service made survival of these lines increasingly difficult, the Southwold being the first to go in 1929. Other closures followed: Campbeltown & Macrihanish in 1932, Leek & Manifold (1934), Glyn Valley Tramway and Lynton & Barnstaple (1935) and Rye & Camber (1939). Swimming against the tide of progress were the Welsh Highland and Ashover Railways, opened in 1923 and 1925 respectively. The former lost money from the start and closed in 1937 but the Ashover became the victim of its own success. Within two years of opening its healthy passenger traffic was seized by a newly started bus service, and regular passenger services ended in 1931, although excursions were run subsequently. Lime-

A 'real photographic' card published as part of the publicity drive following the Festiniog Railway's lease of the Welsh Highland Railway in 1934. Tan-y-Bwlch station mistress Bessie Jones hands the single line token to MERDDIN EMRYS' driver.

stone ballast workings lasted until 1950. Only three lines in mainland Britain survived intact: the Talyllyn (which never closed) and two other lines which, having come under G.W.R. control, passed to British Railways' ownership in 1948 – the Vale of Rheidol (still operated by B.R. today) and the Welshpool and Llanfair, closed by B.R. in 1956 but later reopened by a preservation society.

The narrow gauge railway could conquer territory that no standard gauge line would attempt. The 1'11½" gauge Vale of Rheidol Railway used conventional methods to take passengers from sea level at Aberystwyth to 600 feet at Devil's Bridge. However the 3,500 foot height of Snowdon required application of Swiss technology to produce Britain's only 'rack and pinion' railway (2'7½" gauge) which opened in 1897. Island railways developed separately, the 3'0" gauge system

A delightful scene on the 15" gauge Romney Hythe and Dymchurch Railway, carefully posed to emulate the famous Southern Railway publicity poster. A black and white card published by R.A. Postcards, London EC4.

on the Isle of Man (1873) being the first large scale application of narrow gauge outside North Wales. Only the Douglas–Port Erin section now survives, together with the 3'0" gauge Manx Electric Railway (Douglas–Ramsey) and the 3'6" gauge line to Snaefell summit. The Channel Islands generally opted for standard gauge, except for the 3'6" gauge Jersey Railway (a mere 8½ miles in length) which closed in 1936.

In Ireland, Governmental influence ensured 'standardisation' on the 3'0" gauge for secondary railways, thanks to the 1883 Tramways Act which provided financial guarantees to promoters of such lines. Eventually some 560 miles of 3'0" gauge railway were constructed. Most were local lines serving places of little importance – an exception being the Cork and Muskerry which carried substantial tourist traffic to Blarney. Only in the remote North West did narrow gauge railways combine to form a major system, the Londonderry and Lough Swilly and County Donegal together owning over 220 miles of track. Even here, however, non-standardisation of couplings and buffer heights prevented interchange of locos and rolling stock. All public Irish narrow gauge lines are now closed, the last survivor (the West Clare) closing in 1961.

The military was an early user of narrow gauge railways. Following the success of the 18" gauge system at the L.N.W.R. Crewe works, from 1871 a line of this gauge was laid down at the Royal Arsenal, Woolwich, becoming the most extensive industrial railway in the country. Later various naval depots were (some still are) served by narrow gauge railways, generally of 2'6" gauge, while the Army and RAF used 2'0" gauge.

But the greatest use of military railways was on the actual battlefield. After a few abortive experiments with temporary light railways in various Colonial wars the British Army went back to their traditional horsedrawn transport. Not so the French and Germans who developed extensive 60cm. gauge railways to serve their frontier fortifications. In World War 1, the stalemate of trench warfare, the constant shelling and torrential rain soon reduced the ground to a sea of mud impassable by road transport. By 1916 Britain had joined the other adversaries in laying down a very extensive network of temporary 60cm. gauge railways, using portable track sections of the 'Decauville' system developed 30 years earlier.

Apart from the railways built at home, British engineers were responsible for the design and construction of railways all over the globe. The locomotives, rolling stock and materials for these were almost exclusively made at home. Among the locomotive builders concentrating on this sector of the market were Manning Wardle, Hunslet Engine Co., and Hudswell Clarke, all situated in close proximity in Jack Lane, Leeds, and W.G. Bagnall at Stafford. Whilst the Leeds firms concentrated purely on building locomotives, Bagnalls and their local rivals Kerr Stuart of Stoke-on-Trent also built a range of narrow gauge rolling stock and trackwork. Both Bagnall and Hudswell Clarke were early pioneers in the development of internal combustion engined locomotives, Bagnall building their first petrol locomotives in 1912, while Hudswells produced the first conventional diesel locomotive in Britain as early as 1927. They later (1946 onwards) specialised in the production of flame-proofed underground mines locomotives.

The geographic and economic influences which caused narrow gauge railways to develop at home were also present in Europe, and every European country had its quota of n.g. railways. France had a vast network of 'secondaires' (almost all metre gauge) serving largely agricultural areas. These lines were a source of considerable local pride and until recently picture postcards of the local 'tortillard' were commonly to be found in many village shops. Belgium too had an extensive secondary system, the 'Vicinal' with over 5,000 km of mostly metre gauge. In most Western European countries, the narrow gauge railway has largely disappeared. Exceptions are Spain and Portugal, with large metre gauge networks in the north, and Switzerland, where mountain railways were built to open up areas of the country inaccessible by road or conventional railway.

Outside Europe and North America, 'narrow gauge' is a term with a wider range of meanings. In India, the British administration chose 5'6" gauge as 'standard' but also created a large network of metre gauge lines. Many 2'0" and 2'6" gauge lines were also built, often as a result of private enterprise by the Princely states. In South America and Australia, railways of metre and 3'6" gauges supplemented broad or standard gauge networks and extended to thousands of miles. In Africa, imperial rivalries and geographic considerations produced a proliferation of gauges, of which the "Cape" gauge of 3'6" was the most popular. Locomotives and rolling stock on these railways were often built to 'main line' proportions (sometimes exceeding the UK loading gauge) and as such fall outside the usual definition of narrow gauge.

This 'real photographic' card from an anonymous publisher is an impressive study of the two Bullock 4-6-4's at the terminus of the 12¼" gauge Littlehampton Miniature Railway in Sussex.

A general view of Ballinamore station, head-quarters of the Cavan and Leitrim Railway in Eire. Cards like this include valuable details of track layouts, station 'furniture' and railway architecture, much of the latter now irretrievably lost.

The fifteen inch gauge has two separate (but interconnected) origins. Originator of the 15" gauge in a load-carrying capacity was Sir Arthur Heywood, an amateur engineer who calculated 15" to be the 'minimum gauge' for carriage of goods and passengers while gaining the maximum economies in construction and material. His own Duffield Bank Railway (built 1874-81) proved the concept, and Heywood devoted his life to promoting the 15" gauge for agricultural and estate use. One such line was constructed, under Heywood's supervision, on the Duke of Westminster's Eaton Hall estate near Chester in 1895-6.

The first move in encouraging the wider popularity of the 15" gauge came when Mr Charles Bartholomew (a contemporary of Heywood) built an 'Eaton Hall' style railway on his estate at Blakesley Hall, Northants, but operated it with 'true scale' steam and petrol locomotives. The resulting economies in construction and operation stimulated other operators to construct 15" gauge lines for enter-tainment and profit. Most famous was the model engineering firm of W.J. Bassett-Lowke who opened 15" gauge lines at Blackpool (1905), Birmingham (1907), Halifax (1910) and Rhyl (1911). A similar operation, Llewellyn's miniature railway at Southport, also opened in 1911. Following a change in policy Bassett-Lowkes (through their associate Narrow Gauge Railways Ltd.) sought permanent sites for more ambitious 15" gauge lines, and took over the Ravenglass and Eskdale, which had closed down as a 3'0" gauge opera-tion in 1912. Regauged to 15", it reopened in 1915. Original motive power comprised secondhand Heywood locomotives plus a scale model Pacific and Atlantic, designed by Henry Greenly and marking a drift back from 'true scale' designs to motive power of more 'narrow gauge' capability. Another N.G.R. venture was the Fairbourne Railway, opened in 1916 using the trackbed of a former horse worked tramway.

The pinnacle of 15" gauge development came in 1927 with the opening of the Romney, Hythe and Dymchurch Light Railway. Built from scratch in an area neglected by the main line railways, the RH&DR was laid out on a grand scale by its designers to permit the operation of realistically long trains at scale speeds. Local freight traffic was negligible but the load-carrying capacity of the 15" gauge was demonstrated by the carriage of shingle for sale as ballast. The Ravenglass and Eskdale too interspersed the running of passenger trains with 'general' freight traffic and the transport of granite from Beckfoot quarry.

The definition of what is a miniature railway is a wide one, and successful applications of miniature railway engineering (for passenger carrying purposes) exist on gauges from as little as five inches to two feet. Some early miniature railways were privately owned, and rarely open to the public. Others, such as the ambitious Surrey Border and Camberley Railway (10¼" gauge) were commercial ventures. What most miniature railways have in common is their ephemeral nature, being readily transportable to a new site to meet the needs of the owner. With few interested enthusiasts to record these developments, miniature railways are the least documented aspect of railway operation in Great Britain. Fortunately miniature railways do attract the general public, and consequently are often the subject of picture postcards, which in some cases repre-sent the only permanent record of a railway's existence.

RAILWAYS AND POSTCARDS

In this volume it is not possible to do more than touch upon the development of the picture postcard as a medium of communication: readers interested in this aspect are referred to the Bibliography, page 60. However a brief outline of the picture postcard as a subject for collecting is relevant to what follows. Follow ing relaxation of the postal regulations in 1902, there was a boom in postcard sending and collecting which (at times) seemed to consume the energies of the entire nation. Adults and children alike built up collec-tions, and publishers churned out cards by the million to meet the demand. The hobby was dealt a severe blow by the doubl-ing of the postage rates (from ½d to 1d) in 1918, and the boom was over. Many collections were discarded, but one expert has calculated that even if 99% of the postcards produced between 1902 and 1918 have been destroyed, there are still 100,000,000 in existence!

In 1896 a magazine devoted to railways was published for the first time. 'Moore's Monthly Magazine' (which preceded the Railway Magazine by a year) subsequently became 'The Locomotive' and the publishers produced their first postcards in 1898. These early cards, following the fashion of the time, were printed in full colour from artist-drawn paintings (them-selves often 'inspired' by a photograph). The Locomotive Publishing Co. (LPC) published cards under their own name

An interesting example of an 'official' postcard: the Lincolnshire Coast Light Railway opened in 1960 and featured a maker's photograph of their Peckett 0-6-0ST JURASSIC as the centrepiece of this card.

and under that of F. Moore, the pseudonym of their house artist Thomas Rudd.

Non-specialist publishers too were quick to see the appeal of railway subjects to postcard collectors generally. Raphael Tuck & Co. published the first of their 'Famous Express Trains of the World' series in 1906 and a series of 'London Railway Stations' in 1907. Valentine's of Dundee published similar series of 'Famous Railway Engines' and 'Express Trains'. The newsagents W.H. Smith had close connections with railways, and they published postcards of railway stations which are much sought after today.

A prime use of the postcard was as a cheap advertising medium and many pre-Grouping Railway Companies produced their own cards which are known as 'officials'. However not all these feature railways: some show only views of towns or countryside served by the Railway concerned. Occasionally the Railway's territory is interpreted liberally, for example the L.N.W.R. featured views of the (independent) Festiniog Railway as one of their 'officials'! Oddly, the 'old' Festiniog Railway Co. was known only to publish one official card, but officials were published by, among others, the Corris Railway, the Snowdon Mountain Tramroad, the Lynton and Barnstaple and the (post-1915) Ravenglass and Eskdale Railways.

Even after the end of the 'Golden Age' of postcard collecting after 1920, steadily growing interest in railways as a hobby ensured that postcards featuring railways continued to be issued, although on a reduced scale. Again, growing middle class affluence (and mobility) in the 1930's injected new life into some minor railways fortunate enough to be in holiday areas, consequently such railways featured on countless 'commercial' postcards.

There has always been a steady market for black and white postcards of locomotives, trains and stations, produced by the photographic rather than printing process (thus ensuring higher quality and greater exclusivity), such cards being known as 'real photographic' (RP). These, although produced on card with a 'Postcard' back, were primarily intended to be collected rather than sent through the post. Large numbers were produced by LPC (see above) and the Locomotive & General Railway Publishing Co. (L&GRP) from the early part of the century up to the 1960's. Other companies in this field included Ian Allan Ltd., Norman Kerr and Lens of Sutton — the latter still trading under their original name and still producing photographic cards.

To bring the story up to date, the 'new' narrow gauge and preservation societies which sprang up following the rescue of the Talyllyn Railway in 1951 realised the publicity and revenue-earning value of postcards, and many attractive real photographic and printed cards were issued in the 1950's and early 1960's. Cards showing these railways in their early 'preservation' days are highly collectable as they show the railways in a very different form to which they have evolved today.

Most private or enthusiast-run railways now produce their own postcards, but ironically the increase in quantity has been matched by a diminution in quality. Technological 'progress' in the printing industry has enabled three-colour printed cards to be churned out in vast quantities at a few pence each, consequently the black and white photographic card has been priced off the mass market and is all but extinct. The modern range of picture postcards, printed in lurid colours, and often to the larger 'Continental' size (148mm x 105mm) is not of interest to the majority of serious collectors.

Drawing on these various sources, this book sets out to illustrate the rise, development and heyday of the narrow gauge and miniature railway, as seen on the picture postcard. It is a fascinating story and one which, as the current postcard collecting boom unearths new cards, is only just beginning.

AUTHOR'S NOTE

In compiling a book of this kind an inevitable limitation is imposed by the availability of space. No attempt has been made to feature every narrow gauge line: the criteria for inclusion have invariably been the quantity, quality and interest of available views. The aim has been to provide a wide coverage of the diversity of narrow gauge and miniature railways and at the same time to provide a representative cross-section of the postcard Publisher's art.

In preparing the captions I have assumed a degree of basic knowledge on the part of the reader with (at the very least) the best known of the railways featured. Essential data about all the railways featured is summarised at Appendix 1 and, for those who wish to know more, a 'selective bibliography' is provided (page 60).

The postcards have been credited to the original Publishers where known: details are at Appendix 2. In some cases this has unfortunately not been possible, due for example to failure of the Publisher to show his name on the card.

ACKNOWLEDGEMENTS

We gratefully acknowledge the assistance of the following individuals for providing information and/or advice: Alan Burgess, Keith Stretch, Hugh Hughes, M.G. Shelmore, D. Brooks, A.T. Warwick, J.S. Berry, Mike Jackson, Brian Hilton, W.J.K. Davies, D.H. Smith, Ron Cox, Dave Holroyde, Ron Redman, Mike Swift, Ian Miller.

Special thanks are due to the various Publishers for making available copyright material: E.T.W. Dennis & Sons Ltd.; Ian Allan Ltd.; Ravenglass & Eskdale Railway Co Ltd.; Talyllyn Railway Co; Welshpool & Llanfair Light Railway Preservation Co; and particularly to Valentine's of Dundee Ltd for their generous assistance.

The postcards were copied for publication by Brookside Photographic Services, Shrewsbury, and the cover artwork is by Mary Males.

SLATE, STONE and ORE

LOADING STONE, PENMAENMAWR QUARRIES

1

(1) The earliest steam locomotives associated with the North Wales quarries were the four-coupled vertical boilered machines locally built by DeWinton & Co. at Caernarvon. Crude and cheap, they were ideally suited to the rough quarry tracks and primitive maintenance facilities and some lasted into the 1950's. This scene depicted on a 'Renshaw' series card was photographed around 1905 on the Graiglwyd gallery of Darbishire's Ltd's Penmaenmawr Granite quarries and shows one of the firm's five DeWinton locos (probably LILLIAN) about to pull away from the crushing plant with a load of stone. Darbishire's and the adjacent quarries of Brundrit and Co. Ltd. (the two amalgamated in 1911) used 3'0" gauge, rather than the more common 2'0", for their railways, which were replaced with dumper trucks and conveyor belts in 1967.   (2) Portmadoc Harbour station on the Festiniog Railway circa 1902 with double Fairlie MERDDIN EMRYS still very much as built about to depart with a mixed train of bogie and four wheel passenger coaches. Note the harbour crowded with coastal schooners all engaged in shipping slate brought down from Blaenau Festiniog by the Railway.

Festiniog Railway, Portmadoc

2

3

Best known of the slate quarry railways were the extensive 1'10¾" inch gauge sytems of Penrhyn Quarries, Bethesda and Dinorwic Quarries,Llanberis, which closed in 1964 and 1969 respectively. (3) and (4) show relatively recent views of these systems. (3) This view issued as a Real Photographs card was taken in the 1950's, one of a series depicting slate quarry locomotives. A gleaming BLANCHE (Hunslet (0-4-OST) has arrived at Bethesda with a train of empties from Port Penrhyn, seven miles away. Following the Penrhyn main line's closure in 1962, BLANCHE and her sister LINDA were sold to the Festiniog and are still at work today.   (4) Within the quarries were fleets of little cabless Hunslet saddletanks, each gallery (quarry level) having its own engine, which would be taken up the connecting cable incline in pieces, then re-assembled and put to work. This picture shows driver Jack Hughes and his mate easing Dinorwic's DOLBADARN and its train of waste trucks along the Bonc Fawr gallery only weeks before withdrawal in 1966. This b/w card was one of a series published by the Maid Marian Locomotive Fund to help save a sister loco at Dinorwic from the scrap heap.

4

PORTMADOC. WELSH HIGHLAND & FESTINIOG RAILWAYS   59830.

5

In the brief period of optimism following the opening of the Welsh Highland Railway through to Portmadoc in June 1923, a combined service was run with the Festiniog and there was a burst of publicity to advertise this. Naturally this included postcards, (5) is one of at least four sepia cards produced by Photochrom Ltd. A train was specially posed at Portmadoc harbour for their photographer Mr. Bucknall with MERDDIN EMRYS (seen above) at the head. Another card in the series (59827) shows PALMERSTON with the empty stock and the Fairlie at the rear. At the time of the combined service, passenger trains would stop at this point, and then (bypassing Harbour station) ran through the streets of Portmadoc, across the G.W.R. line to the bleak WHR station Portmadoc (New) and ultimately on to Beddgelert or Dinas.   (6) An early J. Arthur Dixon colour card of the revived Festiniog Railway. Probably taken in 1958 the year of the re-opening through to Tan-y-Bwlch, PRINCE is shown approaching that station with a train of coaches still in the green and cream livery favoured by the Railway at that time.

6

7

The large number of cards published by the Locomotive Publishing Company under their own name and that of F. Moores are amongst the finest of all railway postcards.   (7) No. 5632 in the F. Moores series shows the Vulcan Foundry 0-6-4T MOEL TRYFAN, one of two such single Fairlies owned by the North Wales Narrow Gauge Railway Co., outside the loco shed at Dinas Junction about 1904. The NWNGR had a short and troubled life, and was later reborn as the Welsh Highland, whose troubles were greater and life correspondingly shorter. Another major slate carrying railway was the Talyllyn, which like the Festiniog found salvation in seasonal passenger traffic as the slate traffic dwindled.   (8) is a classic view of No. 1 TALYLLYN taking water at Dolgoch station in pre-preservation days. This Frith's card was posted in Towyn on 12 August 1929 and the passengers' dress indicates it was probably produced not much earlier. Remarkably, the entire railway, locomotives, rolling stock and track were hardly altered at all from the opening in 1865 to the Preservation Society takeover in 1951.

Ever since the Preservation Society took over the operation of the line in 1951, they have published postcards of the Railway, these two views are from the original sepia tone set printed for the Society by Friths. (9) TR1 shows DOLGOGH about to leave Wharf station with the inaugural train on Whit Monday 1951. On the left is Society founder (and General manager for the first two years) Tom Rolt (in straw hat) while standing by DOLGOCH Chairman Bill Trinder chats to Pat Garland (Treasurer, back to camera). A couple of minutes later Bill Trinder cut the tape and DOLGOCH stormed away to begin the era of enthusiast run railways. (10) In TR3 DOLGOCH is seen passing quarry siding with the brakevan and one coach on its way back to Towyn. This view typifies the delightfully run down state of the railway when the Society took over.

Both the Corris Railway and Glyn Valley Tramway were originally horseworked roadside lines for mineral traffic only, later reconstructed for passenger traffic with steam locomotives.   (11) Being a pure roadside tramway, the G.V.T. had to enclose the wheels and motion of their three Beyer-Peacock 0-4-2T's in a steel skirt and
they were designed to run cab first. Later (1921) they were joined by a War surplus Baldwin 4-6-OT but road
competition forced closure to passengers in 1933 and to slate and granite traffic two years later.   (12) The
Corris however was fenced off from the road so its locomotives needed no protection. Unlike the Talyllyn
Railway in the nearby valley the Corris was for many years a smartly run and prosperous concern, running
horse then motor buses in conjunction with the Railway. Following the G.W.R. takeover in 1930, the passenger
service soon ceased, thereafter only a daily goods for the slate quarries operated. In this RP card published by
Brockham Museum No. 3 is seen pausing at Corris in August 1939 on its way up to Aberllefeni to collect the
day's freight.

THE RURAL RAILWAY

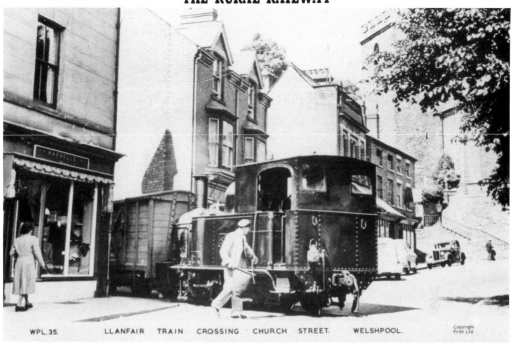

WPL. 35.   LLANFAIR   TRAIN   CROSSING   CHURCH   STREET.   WELSHPOOL.   Copyright Frith Ltd.

Two cards illustrating the Welshpool and Llanfair Railway in its last days as a 'common carrier' and in the early preservation era: (13) Friths card No. WPL 35 shows the fireman of the daily freight train flagging it across Church Street, Welshpool as it returns from Llanfair sometime between 1951 and 1956 – the period during which both locos THE EARL and THE COUNTESS ran without nameplates. Sepia, black and white and colour tinted versions of this card exist, the latter still on sale in Welshpool in 1979, 20 years since trains last crossed the street!   (14) is one of the second (un-numbered) series of officials published by the Preservation Society. Beyer Peacock 0-6-OT THE COUNTESS is seen running alongside the River Banwy with a train for Llanfair. The picture was taken in 1964, a year after re-opening, when all the passenger stock in use had been acquired from the former Chattenden and Upnor Railway operated by the Admiralty in Kent.

(15) The 3'0" gauge Southwold Railway which connected the G.E.R. main line at Halesworth with the sleepy little Suffolk coast resort of Southwold typified the rural English light railway. Bedevilled by a legal speed restriction of 15 mph and the need to tranship freight to the standard gauge at Halesworth, at the first sign of motor bus competition its owners threw in the towel and the line closed in April 1929. This picture issued recently as a Photomatic card was taken in Edwardian days when the little Sharp Stewart 2-4-OT BLYTHE and the staff at Southwold could pose proudly for the camera with no worries about redundancy.   (16) Scotland's only public narrow gauge line ran from Macrihanish across to Campbeltown harbour down in the Mull of Kintyre. Reconstructed from an earlier 2'3" gauge colliery line in 1906, it relied heavily on the colliery for its existence and when that shut, the railway followed soon after in 1932. Due to its remoteness few enthusiasts were able to visit and photograph it, but a few postcards were produced by local Photographer/Publishers, including this one showing one of the Barclay 0-6-2T's and train on Campbeltown quay.

Campbeltown and Machrihanish Railway

The jibe that the Leek and Manifold Valley Light Railway 'began nowhere and ended up the same place' was cruelly true, for beautiful as the Valley was it yielded precious little traffic. Hopes of a copper mining revival came to nothing, the railway having to rely on milk traffic, plus tourists in the season. Despite this the Railway was a wonderful tribute to its designer E.R. Calthrop. Locomotives and coaches were directly based on his previous project, the 2'6" gauge Barsi Light Railway in India. The North Staffordshire Railway worked hard to attract traffic to the line, devoting 8 of its 23 official postcard sets to it.   (17) shows the first train to reach Hulme End, on 23 May 1904, behind No. 1 E.R. CALTHROP, one of two identical Kitson 2-6-4T's.   (18) depicts the line between Thors Cave and Redhurst Crossing, a view actually taken before the line's official opening, the subject of the photo being an inspection train. This photo originally taken for LPC was also issued by the Alphalsa Publishing Co., and cards issued after 1923 had 'North Stafford Railway' replaced by 'London Midland and Scottish Railway.'

River Manifold near Thor's Cave. North Stafford Railway

No book on narrow gauge railways could fail to feature the delightful Lynton and Barnstaple Railway, but coverage of the Railway on postcards is mostly confined to the series of officials beautifully printed for the L & B by the Pictorial Stationery Co. in their Peacock 'Autochrom' series, plus sundry enthusiasts' postcards. (19) Friths did feature the line however, their No. 59449 shows a train from Lynton climbing the steep grade through Barbrook woods to the summit near Woody Bay station. The extra work caused by unexpected rock on this section caused the bankruptcy of James Nuttall, the contractor who built the line.   (20) Originally the four locomotives were simply named after local rivers, EXE, LYN, TAW AND YEO, but following absorbtion into the Southern Railway in 1923, all four were numbered into the LSWR locomotive series and later as they became due for repainting, the word SOUTHERN in six inch primrose lettering was added to their tank sides. EXE is seen in this final livery at Barnstaple Town around 1930.

The Southern Railway took its responsibilities to the L & B very seriously, spending much money on track, buildings and stock. This included a fourth Manning Wardle 2-6-2T LEW, seen here with a works train at Bratton Fleming about 1929. The train includes a bogie open wagon by Howerd's of Bedford, one of eight new wagons purchased in 1927. The loop and one siding were removed in February 1932, but by then the line was beyond mere economy measures and closed completely on September 29th, 1935.   (22) Swords into ploughshares . . . . the Ashover Light Railway bought six Baldwin 4-6-OT's and 70 Hudson bogie wagons from ex First World War stock to work its line and later acquired several petrol electric locos from the same source. On this real photographic card a Baldwin waits at Ashover Butts terminus for passengers to join its short train around 1925. The left hand coach was acquired from the Wembley Exhibition 'Neverstop Railway'. It and its companion, built new by Gloucester Carriage & Wagon Co. Ltd., are both mounted on ex WD bogies to save money.

The Light Railway Ashover.

23

(23) The Sand Hutton Light Railway started life as a 15″ gauge pleasure railway on Sir Robert Walker's Estate at Sand Hutton, near York. After World War 1 it was decided to expand the railway to carry both freight and passengers, and availability of secondhand locomotives from Deptford Meat Depot precipitated a change of gauge to 1′6′ in 1922. Several picture postcards of the 15″ gauge line exist (see also (71)) but contemporary postcards of the 1′6″ gauge line are elusive. However this November 1927 view of Claxton brickworks produced as a Photomatic card nicely captures the line's 'light railway' atmosphere. (24) The Rye and Camber Tramway in Sussex subsisted entirely on passengers, most of them seasonal, and in its latter days was operated by only one man. The economy was achieved by substituting this neat little petrol locomotive, locally built in Ashford by the Kent Construction and Engineering Co., for the original two Bagnall 2-4-OT's. In this 1930's view by a local Publisher such a train prepares to leave Rye with the entire passenger stock, benches being put in two open wagons when things really got busy.

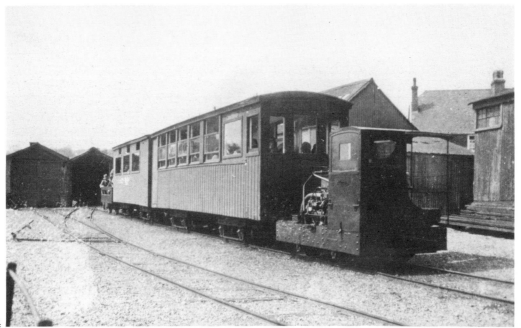

24

AROUND THE ISLANDS

The 3'0" gauge Isle of Man Railway remained unchanged for almost 100 years: opened in 1873, by the 1950's it was a 'time capsule' of a working Victorian railway.   (25) Most postcards featured the Douglas terminus, which makes this Photomatic view of No. 6 PEVERIL at St Johns on 17 May 1956 especially valuable. St Johns was the junction for Ramsey and Peel and the single coach and van is probably the Peel portion of a Peel and Ramsey – Douglas working. Soon afterwards a decline set in, and the whole Railway closed in November 1965. A group of businessmen chaired by Lord Ailsa took over the Railway and intitially re-opened the Douglas – Peel line on 3rd June 1967.   (26) Some real photographic cards were published by the IOM Railway Association to publicise the re-opening and this one shows Douglas station with several of the Beyer Peacock 2-4-OT's decked with flags for the occasion. The locos are Nos. 5, 10, 12, 11 and (nearest camera) NO. 8 FENELLA. Regrettably the bold scheme failed and both the Peel and Ramsey lines closed permanently in 1968.

Derby Castle Tramway Station, Douglas, Isle of Man

27

The Manx Electric Railway has probably changed less than any other line illustrated in this book. Nationalised on 1 June 1957, the 22½ miles of double track electrified railway maintained an all year round 'common carrier' service up to September 1975 when economic pressures forced the abandonment of winter services and closure of the Laxey – Ramsey section. Fortunately the IOM Government found more cash and after a summer of Douglas – Laxey only operation, the line opened on a summer basis in 1977. Our two cards are from an earlier, more prosperous era.   (27) Boots (the Chemists) were originally 'Cash Chemists and Stationers' and naturally published their own postcards, including the 'Pelham' series, No. 595 of which shows the MER Douglas terminus at Derby Castle just after the turn of the Century. The poster (left) quotes fares of 1/6d to Laxey and 2/6d to Ramsey, but if fares, road vehicles and some surrounding buildings have changed, the railway itself hasn't. Indeed the only reason one cannot repeat this 1905 view (28) of a Ramsey train crossing Ballure viaduct is the increased growth of trees, the rest is just the same.

Manx Electric Railway - Crossing Ballure Bridge

28

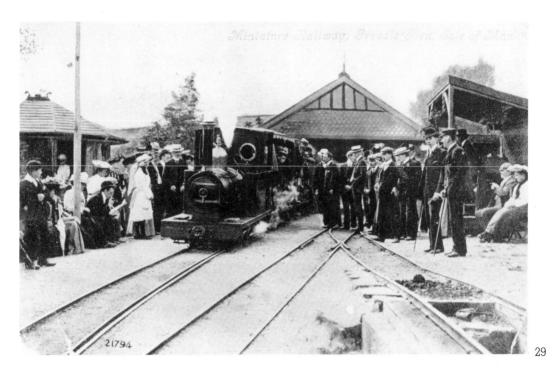

29

(29) Opening day on the Groudle Glen Railway, IOM, on 23 May 1896 with diminutive Bagnall 2-4-OT SEA LION about to depart with the first train. A second locomotive POLAR BEAR arrived in 1905, the names chosen after the animals kept in a rock pool at the seaward end of the ¾ mile long line. After a brief unsuccesful experiment with battery locomotives in the 1920's, the line staggered on with no renewals of stock or track until a combination of chronic neglect and vandalism forced closure in 1962. Happily, both locos were rescued for preservation.   (30) The original Jersey Railway from St Helier to St Aubin was standard gauge and opened in 1870 but the extension to Corbiere finished 13 years later was built to 3'6" gauge and the original line regauged to suit. Never a financial success, it eventually closed after a disastrous fire at St Aubin station in 1936. In happier days, Bagnall 2-4-OT No. 3 CORBIERE prepares to leave St Aubin on a summer day in 1913. This view is by the French publisher Louis Levy whose prolific output in the years 1900 – 1920 included many views of the Channel Islands and Southern England.

30

31

When the London and North Western Railway reached Llanberis in 1869 their immediate ambition was to construct an extension to the summit of Snowdon. In the event it was an independent company, the Snowdon Mountain Tramroad and Hotels Co., which built the 800mm gauge line, using the swiss Abt rack system. Nevertheless the LNWR was astute enough to feature the line on one of its official cards (31). The view shown is a strange choice, the picture having been taken before the formal opening of the railway and, tragically, on the opening day (Easter Monday 1896) an identical two coach train, propelled by this same SLM-built 0-4-2T LADAS came to grief when the loco jumped the track and was completely destroyed.   (32) This Valentine's card shows the Railway in more normal operation before 1910: No 4 SNOWDON pauses at Clogwyn awaiting clearance to proceed. SNOWDON, one of the second batch of SLM tanks with enlarged dome, was taken out of service in 1939 and remained derelict until rebuilt by Hunslets, Leeds in 1961-3.

Vale of Rheidol Railway.

The Vale of Rheidol Railway opened in 1902, originally to serve metal mines around Devil's Bridge. However tourist traffic to the nearly Mynach Falls quickly became the line's staple business. (33) No. 2 PRINCE OF WALES is seen in the upper valley (at a favourite spot for postcard publishers) en route for Devil's Bridge between 1902 and 1908. No. 2 bears her original 'khaki' livery, replaced in 1908 by a more ornate lined green. These 2-6-2T's bear a close similarity to the Manning Wardle tanks built a few years earlier for the Lynton and Barnstaple Railway, indeed it was suggested that the original Mannings drawings were closely studied by the builders, Davies and Metcalfe. This similarity was cleverly exploited by the publishers of this card, Pictorial Stationery Co., who reissued the card with the caption "Lynton and Barnstaple Railway"! Doubtless few visitors to the L & B spotted the deception. (34) shows Devil's Bridge in the early 1900's when the goods yard was still in use for timber traffic. Whilst the carriage of copper and lead ores had almost finished by 1914, timber remained an important source of traffic for much longer, except in high summer when the timber wagons were converted into extra coaches.

39591. ABERYSTWYTH: RHEIDOL VALLEY, DEVIL'S BRIDGE STATION.

MAINLY FOR PLEASURE

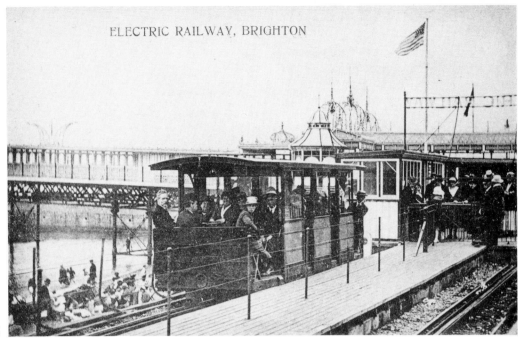

ELECTRIC RAILWAY, BRIGHTON

35

Two cards showing railways that fulfil a 'pure' transport function but which also have a substantial 'pleasure' role.   (35) The Volks Electric Railway was the first successful application of electric rail traction in Britain and (at 103 years) is the oldest surviving electric railway in the world. Originally running from Brighton Palace Pier to Banjo Groyne it was later extended to Black Rock (1¼ miles). This sepia card depicts the original Palace Pier terminus (the line was cut back slightly to terminate at Aquarium in 1933) and features a good close up of one of the historic cars, designed and built by Magnus Volk from 1884 onwards.   (36) Few passengers who ride the little electric train along Hythe Pier to catch the ferry across to Southampton will be aware of its sinister origins. A pair of Brush electric locos have operated the 2'0" gauge third rail electric line since 1922 but were originally built in 1917 for work in the mustard gas factory at Avonmouth. They were converted from battery to third rail drive at Hythe, and are some of the oldest electric locos still at work in Britain.

1199   ELECTRIC TRAIN, HYTHE PIER.

THE MINIATURE RAILWAY, TRENTHAM GARDENS, STAFFORDSHIRE.   K.6273.

The two cards on this page both published around 1950 depict pleasure railways which utilise commercial 2'0" gauge railway equipment, though in both cases it was bought new for the railway concerned. (37) During the depressed 1930's E.E. Baguley Ltd. of Burton-on-Trent helped to make ends meet by building a number of locomotives for various parks, these were mechanically based on the petrol locos they had built for the military in World War 1 but with 'steam outline' bodywork. One such railway (still running today) is at Trentham Gardens near Stoke, with three of these locomotives. Here BRORA built in 1930 hauls a heavily loaded train of Baguley built stock into the station at Trentham.   (38) By contrast the Planet petrol loco supplied by F.C. Hibberd to the Drusillas Zoo line at Berwick, East Sussex in 1946 is a completely standard example of that builder's 'Y Type' loco. Powered by an E93A engine as in a contemporary Ford Prefect car, it has now been displaced by a Ruston diesel. On this line the coaches are built on Hudson 1 cubic yard side tipper underframes.

The Railway, Drusillas, Berwick.   T.S. BWK 34

39

Locomotive builders W.G. Bagnall Ltd. of Stafford produced about 120 advertising cards of locos built bet-ween 1905 and 1950, and three of the cards in this group are taken from that series.   (39) SANTA THEREZA (Bagnall 1906 of 1909) was a typical 'Colonial' narrow gauge locomotive for a 75 cm gauge line in Brazil. Note the open cab and bunker racks for wood or bagasse (cane waste) fuel. Amazingly she was still at work 70 years later, though substantially rebuilt.   (40) The classic Bagnall narrow gauge design was this 0-4-OST with inside frames, outside cylinders and motion and marine pattern boiler with circular steel firebox. Several hun-dred of various sizes and gauges varying between 1'6" and 4'0" were built from 1897 to 1953, Bagnall 2058 is one of the larger variant with 7" by 12" cylinders. One of three 3'0" gauge examples built for Government Forestry work in 1918, 2058 was used on two different Northumberland timber lines until 1925 and then worked at the Consett Iron Co.'s Butsfield Quarry in Co. Durham until scrapping in 1951. Bagnalls incorrectly num-bered this card 2081, the first of a further six locos built for Forestry work in 1918.

(41) Poor old DENNIS, a chunky 0-6-OT built in 1906 (Bagnall 1706) for the Snailbeach District Railway, a mineral line in the Shropshire hills, met a sad end. Following the line's takeover by that redoubtable collector of moribund railways, Lt. Colonel H.F. Stephens, the railway was almost entirely operated by a single employee, a Mr. Gatford. For 25 years he ran the line singlehanded with little outside help and even less money, but unfortunately he didn't like DENNIS! First he simply never used her, then under the pretext of an overhaul she was slowly taken apart and one by one her parts were 'lost' until by 1938 only a solitary pair of wheels remained.   (42) Unlike Bagnalls, Hudswell Clarke limited their advertising cards to the small number of internal combustion and battery electric locomotives produced between the Wars. The only known exception, illustrated on this card, is PIONEER, their very first underground mines locomotive. Built in 1946, it spent all its life on the 3'6" gauge system at Moor Green Colliery, Notts until recently rescued for preservation by the Leeds Industrial Museum.

HUDSWELL CLARKE & CO. LTD., Railway Foundry, LEEDS 10
Locomotive Engineers

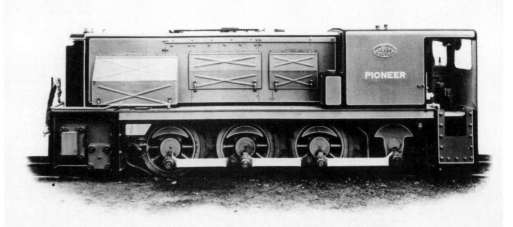

"HUWOOD-HUDSWELL" MINES TYPE DIESEL LOCOMOTIVE
100 H.P.   GAUGES 1' 11½" to 3' 6"   WEIGHT 15 TONS IN W.O.

CORK AND MUSKERRY LIGHT RAILWAY.

324.

By *The Locomotive Publishing Company, Ltd., London.*

43

(43) It must surely have been a summer Sunday when LPC's photographer visited the Cork and Muskerry Light Railway. Even in Edwardian days only an excursion to Blarney would justify such a lengthy train as No. 7 PEAKE is shown hauling along the Leemount road out of Cork. The line never paid its way, competition from buses and trams forcing its closure in 1934. Two locomotives and some rolling stock saw further service on other Irish n.g. lines, but PEAKE, built by Brush Electrical Engineering in 1897, went straight to the scrap heap. (44) The four locomotives from Cork's other 3'0" gauge line, the Cork, Blackrock and Passage, were luckier, being transferred to the Cavan and Leitrim Railway in 1932, following the Cork line's closure. This colour tinted card in the 'Gems of Irish Transport' series shows one of them on a mixed train at Ballyconnel station on the Cavan line sometimes in the 1950's. Note the coach consisting of an old bus body on a railway chassis, an example of the economies forced on the Cavan and Leitrim in its last few years before closure in March 1959.

LOCAL TRAIN AT BALLYCONNELL CO. CAVAN C.I.E.

44

Ireland boasted several 3'0" gauge roadside tramways, the Clogher Valley Railway in Northern Ireland being the longest and possibly the nicest. Running from Maguiresbridge, County Fermanagh for 37 miles to Tynan in County Tyrone it opened in 1887 and survived until 1941. Our three views are all from the L&GRP series, believed to have been taken on one visit in June 1933.   (45) One of the line's original six Sharp Stewart 0-4-2T's ambles into Ballygawley with a short mixed train. Note the cowcatcher and motion side sheeting, also oil lamp and large rear windows – these locos being designed to run cab first to comply with Board of Trade regulations.   (46) Locomotive sheds are rare subjects indeed for postcards – this is Aughnacloy with No. 3 BLACKWATER and another Sharp Stewart on the left, and the ill-fated BLESSINGBOURNE in the centre. Like many another light railway, a small highly skilled staff in the shops worked miracles in the way of repairs with very little proper machinery and even less money. One example of improvisation is the weed spraying wagon in the yard, utilising the old boiler from scrapped No. 1 FURY mounted on open wagon No. 62.

47

(47) Built by Hudswell Clarke in 1907, the Clogher Valley's 0-4-4T BLESSINGBOURNE was a sad failure. Designed by the CVR's engineer, Gustav Akerlind, poor adhesion and a chronically faulty steam brake turned what should have been a more powerful version of the original Sharp Stewarts into a locomotive that pulled less, burned more coal and slipped violently at the least excuse. Cursed by the crews and used as little as possible, she was finally dumped at Aughnacloy in 1927 and scrapped in 1934, a year after this picture was taken.   (48) The County Donegal Railways were not only Ireland's largest 3'0" gauge system, with 124 route miles, but the one that made the most determined efforts to fight off road competition. Under the management first of Henry Forbes and later Bernard Curran it pioneered the use of railcars for lightly used services as early as 1926, and fought hard to retain passenger and freight traffic right up to closure in 1960. Such a large system needed big locomotives, and this 'Gems of Irish Transport' card shows ALICE, one of the powerful 2-6-4T's, in Strabane yard sometime in the 1950's.

NARROW GAUGE AT WAR

Postcards of the 60 cm. gauge War Department Light Railways operated behind the British lines in World War 1 are very scarce.   (49) This photographic card from an anonymous publisher shows the operating staff proudly posing by petrol electric locomotive No. 1908, one of a hundred such machines built by Dick Kerr Ltd. of Preston. The massive Dorman 4J0 engine can clearly be seen under the bonnet. Petrol locomotives were greatly preferred to steam by both sides for this work, as the sparks and smoke from the latter made them an easy target for enemy artillery.   (50) A rare view of a French Army 60 cm. gauge Pechot – Bourdon 0-4-4-0T. Originally designed in 1882 the locomotive was similar to a Fairlie articulated but with only one firebox. Between then and 1906 52 of these machines were built for use behind the border forts on the German frontier and on the extensive military light railways in French Morocco, where this picture was taken. Once the World War started a further 280 were hurridly ordered from Baldwin in the USA plus fifteen from the North British Locomotive Works in Glasgow.

SCENES DE MANŒUVRES - Ravitaillement d'eau par le Decauville

51

The Royal Arsenal at Woolwich boasted the most extensive narrow gauge system in Britain, with 30 miles of 18″ gauge track and another 25 miles mixed with standard gauge. Sadly few enthusiasts were permitted to view it at work but a series of pictures was used to illustrate a lengthy article in the 'Locomotive Magazine' in October/November 1921. Ten of them were issued as real photographic postcards by the Brockham Museum Association in 1964.   (51) Every workshop, store and magazine was served by the railway, was well as a half-hourly workman's passenger service, with stops at ¼ mile intervals. One such passenger train is shown hauled by SHEFFIELD, one of a batch of oil-fired 0-4-OT's built by Avonside in 1916-17.   (52) A selection of 18″ gauge rolling stock is illustrated in this view, which also clearly shows the very substantial trackwork which utilised 56lb/yd rails on the 18″ gauge main line and no less than 105lb rail on the dual gauge track in the foreground.

(53) Woolwich Arsenal again: amongst the seventy 18″ gauge steam locomotives were ten of these pretty little Kerr Stuart saddletanks. POMPEY (delivered in 1912) pauses for the photographer while shunting.   (54) The enormous demand for timber during the 1914-18 War necessitated the setting up of a special department of the Board of Trade to run Forestry operations. Difficulties of access to the often hilly sites meant that temporary light railways normally (but not always) of 3′0″ gauge were built to carry the logs to the nearest sawmill. Most of the workforce were experienced Canadian foresters specially recruited, but German POW's and units of the Womens Land Army were also employed. A group of such workers is seen here alongside a temporary 3′0″ gauge line somewhere in the Scottish Highlands. This real photographic card is number 3 in a series but whether other cards feature railways is not known at this stage.

BEYOND CALAIS...

214   *Chemin de Fer du PUY DE DOME. — L'Arrivée au Sommet (1.465 m.).*   ND. **Phot.**

(55) France had a great number of light and narrow gauge railways. Most found their way onto picture postcards, even this obscure metre gauge line, the C.F. de Puy de Dome, which connected Clermont Ferrand with Puy de Dome summit. Opened in 1907, it closed in 1917 when the rail was requisitioned by the military for use with siege artillery! It re-opened in 1923 but closed finally in 1926. An oddity lay in the use of the 'Systeme Hanscotte', similar to the Fell system using a raised centre rail for both traction and braking, on the upper section of line.   (56) Heavy freight and rush hour passenger traffic plus a dedicated management allowed the 3'6" gauge Rotterdam Steam Tramway to fight off road competition long after all its sister lines had closed, but ultimately defeat came. Partial closure on 1 January 1957 allowed withdrawal of all the delightful steam locos with their wheels and motion hidden behind the statutory steel skirts. However as this Dutch postcard shows, even the diesel locomotives had their own charm, maintaining a service until final closure on 23 September 1965. A short stretch of the line is preserved.

Brielle, Station R.T.M. (Laatste Tramrit 23 sept. 1965)

The Swiss engineer Nicholas Riggenbach took out a patent in 1863 for operating trains up steep gradients, by
equipping the locomotives with vertical toothed wheels ('pinions') driven by separate cylinders, engaging a
steel ladder ('rack') laid between the running lines.   (57) Riggenbach's first 'rack and pinion' railway, the
Vitznau – Rigibahn opened in 1871 from Vitznau to Staffel, was an immediate success and inspired other
similar railways (generally of 80 cm. or metre gauge) throughout Switzerland. Rack railways are well represen-
ted on postcards, this official card shows the Vitznau terminus with a train for the summit awaiting departure
sometime around 1905. Note the angle of the boiler (a design feature to keep the firebox crown sheets covered
on the gradient) and the roads to the loco shed fanning out from the turntable.   (58) On the Portuguese island
of Madeira a metre gauge rack line, built 1891-1912, connected Funchal (Pombal) with Terreiro da Luta
(876m.). Motive power comprised four 0-4-OT's from Maschienenfabrik Esslingen plus one SLM 0-4-2T. This
card shows the section between Pombal and Monte, where the line was paralleled by the famous toboggans
that, alas, have outlasted the railway, which closed in 1942.

Madeira. Elevador do Monte.

59

Two cards which illustrate aspects of the present day narrow gauge scene in Europe.   (59) The narrow gauge lines of East Germany are now almost unique in still being exclusively steam worked but despite that are a model of efficiency with well maintained stock and track, well filled trains and freight mainly carried in standard gauge wagons on transporter cars. This recent view taken on the Freital Hainsberg – Kurort Kipsdorf 750mm gauge line shows a typical LKM built 2-10-2T entering Dippoldiswalde station with a train of loaded transporter cars.   (60) is a timeless scene on the metre gauge Achenseebahn in Austria, connecting Jenbach (near Innsbruck) with the inland lake where passengers change to the company's 'steamer.' The line is operated on the rack system from Jenbach to Eban summit, then by adhesion (the locomotive pulling the train) to Achensee. The line opened in 1889 and has never acquired any new motive power! No. 1 illustrated is one of three Vienna Locomotive Works 0-4-OT's, actually a rebuild combining parts from the original No. 1 and No. 4.

In India, railways serving the hill stations used conventional (adhesion) methods but adopted gradients much steeper than those normally encountered in Britain.   (61) The Matheran Hill Railway climbs 2363 ft. in 13 miles between Neral and Matheran, with a maximum gradient of 1 in 20. This view shows No. 2, one of four large and powerful Orenstein and Koppel 0.6.OT's delivered in 1905-07. The outer axles of these locomotives are hollow, allowing radial movement for negotiating sharp curves.   (62) Most famous of the hill railways, still operating today, is the Darjeeling – Himalaya, an 87 km. long 2'0″ gauge line reaching a maximum height of 7,407 ft. Postcards of the line, especially of the 'loop' section above Tindharia, are not uncommon, however this card depicts a freight train, a rarity on commercial postcards. No. 12A was one of the first ' A series' locomotives, built as 0-4-OWT's in 1881-2 but soon rebuilt with the small saddletank and coal bunkers in front of the cab. Nominally all eight were built by Sharp Stewart, and carry SS plates, however Nos. 11-14 were subcontracted to Hunslets. All except 9 and 10 were withdrawn and replaced by the 'B' class 0-4-OST's by 1911.

DARJEELING. GOODS TRAIN BELOW SONADA.

D 436.

MT. WASHINGTON COG RAILWAY TRAIN, MARSHFIELD STATION, WHITE MTS., N. H.   3A63

63

(63) A pioneer among mountain rack lines, the 4'8" gauge Mount Washington cog railway climbs for 3½ miles to the summit of Mount Washington in New Hampshire at an average grade of 1 in 4, with a maximum of 1 in 2.7 on Jacob's Ladder. Opened in 1869, the line was the creation of Sylvester Marsh, who was forced to spend a night out on the mountain in 1852, and determined to build a railway up the mountain to prevent anyone else repeating his unpleasant experience!   (64) The last large scale usage of steam haulage on industrial narrow gauge lines is in the sugar cane industry in Brazil, the Phillipines, India and particularly Indonesia where even in 1986 hundreds of steam locos remain at work. Sadly these fascinating lines remain largely undocumented by postcard Publishers, an exception being in Australia. Queensland's 2'0" gauge sugar lines are now dieselised, the last steam operation at Victoria mill finishing after the 1976 harvest. On this superb Peer Productions coloured card, HOMEBUSH, an 0-6-0 built by Hudswell Clarke in 1914, is seen hard at work hauling a loaded train of cane cars to the mill.

64

Copyright No. 42   The Gordon Stationery & Bookstores, Khartoum

Khartoum Tram

Interest in railways within Africa has never been great and postcards specifically depicting railways are uncommon. (65) is a Sudanese card depicting the Khartoum 'Tram', originally a 2'0" gauge light railway connecting Khartoum with Omdurman North and Shambat. Opened in 1904 with two Orenstein and Koppel 30 HP 0-4-2T's, motive power had, by 1912, increased to six 30 HP and six 40 HP locos. Most of the line was regauged to 3'6" in 1925 and electrified to form a true tramway but the Shambat line, dieselised in 1934, survived until 1949. (66) The Belgian Congo (now Zaire) had a bizarre collection of 'Colonial' railways, this Belgian card depicts the CF Vicineaux du Mayumbe, a 610mm gauge line connecting the river port of Boma with Lukala and Tchela (137km). First locomotives were eight St. Leonard 0-4-OT's built 1898-99. By 1910 they had been joined by six small Beyer – Garratts (the first of this type to run in Africa) but surprisingly, as late as 1920 (when this card was posted) one of the tiny 0-4-OT's was entrusted with the train 'by which the Minister of Colonies was carried to Mayumbe.'

BOMA.   CONGO-BELGE.

Le Train par lequel M. le Ministre des Colonies s'est rendu au Mayumbe.

FIFTEEN INCHES APART

67 (67) Opened on Whit Monday 1905, the Blackpool Miniature Railway was the first 15" gauge public railway in Great Britain. Bassett-Lowke had started work on LITTLE GIANT in December 1904 and this, their first locomotive, together with four bogie coaches were used to operate the line until its closure and removal to a new site at Halifax Zoo. Miniature Railways of Great Britain Ltd. had been formed by Bassett-Lowke and his associates to build and operate these railways,with Henry Greenly as engineer, this uncredited B/W card is very probably produced by the firm as publicity for the line.   (68) Last and most ambitious project of Miniature Railways Ltd. was the Rhyl Miniature Railway, opened in 1911. This sepia card shows 'Little Giant' GEORGE THE FIFTH which was obtained from the Llewellyn Miniature Railway at Southport. When this loco proved insufficiently powerful, the Railway's engineer Albert Barnes designed a similar but larger locomotive, built to ⅓ scale rather than Little Giant's ¼ scale. Five Barnes Atlantics were built for Rhyl between 1920 and 1934 and a sixth for Dreamland, Margate in 1928.

The Miniature Railway, Marine Lake and Park, Rhyl.
Locomotive built by Messrs. BASSETT-LOWKE, LTD., LONDON & NORTHAMPTON.

One of Britain's earliest 15" gauge lines linked Mr. C.W Bartholomew's home at Blakesley Hall near Towces-
ter, Northants with the local station. Opened in 1903, its prime function was to move coal and other materials to
the house but its owner was also a keen railway enthusiast and ran his line as such. Originally worked by two
American 'Cagney' 4-4-0's, Bartholomew soon turned to internal combustion, building PETROLEA, a 4-4-4
petrol loco in 1905. This being a great success, Bassett-Lowke were prevailed upon to build BLACOLVESLEY,
their first and only petrol locomotive, utilising many 'Little Giant' parts.   (69) Internal combustion locos were
a great novelty at the time and the line was host to a Railway Club visit in June 1914. LPC issued this card of
BLACOLVESLEY with a detailed caption recording that 'the engine will attain a maximum speed of 30
mph.'   (70) shows PETROLEA as rebuilt in 1910 entering Blakesley station. Note the 'V' skip wagons on the
left of which there were five for carrying coal. The railway closed in 1947 although BLACOLVESLEY
survives elsewhere.

71 *The "Eskdale" Miniature Railway,* Ravenglass, Cumberland.

Two interesting examples of deliberate 'deception' by a Publisher. Both cards purport to show the Ravenglass and Eskdale Railway but were taken on other 15″ gauge lines before the Ravenglass line was even built.   (71) This view actually shows Class 30 Bassett-Lowke Atlantic SYNOLDA in service on the Sand Hutton Light Railway (see (23)) in 1913, and to add to the deception it was not SYNOLDA but SANS PAREIL which later worked at Ravenglass!   (72) was taken in 1914 during locomotive trials on the Duke of Westminster's Eaton Hall Railway. Frustrated by lack of space at Staughton Manor, J.E.P. Howey brought his new Bassett Lowke Pacific JOHN ANTHONY to Eaton Hall to try its paces on the much longer line, the locomotive reaching 35 mph. It is shown here with Heywood 0-4-OT KATIE, with driver Harry Wilde on the footplate, Cecil J. Allen (railway journalist) and the Duke standing behind, and Howey in the cab of JOHN ANTHONY. Both photos were probably taken by W.J. Bassett-Lowke himself, who was a keen photographer, and later published as cards to publicise the Eskdale line when it opened in 1915. Both KATIE and JOHN ANTHONY later worked at Ravenglass.

GOODS LOCOMOTIVE "KATIE" BUILT BY THE LATE SIR ARTHUR HEYWOOD, BART.
EXPRESS PASSENGER LOCOMOTIVE "COLOSSUS" BUILT BY BASSETT-LOWKE LTD, LONDON & NORTHAMPTON
ESKDALE NARROW GAUGE RAILWAY, CUMBERLAND.

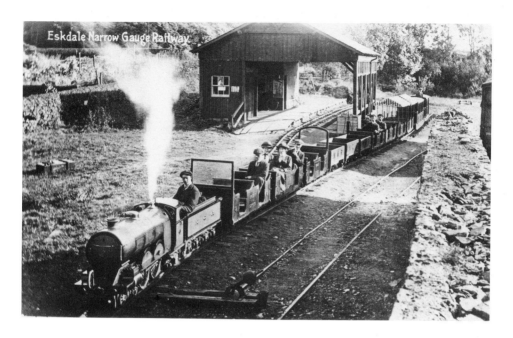

(73) The earliest known postcard of the Ravenglass and Eskdale Railway proper in 15" gauge days is this 1915 picture published by Meckin's Real Photo of Egremont. The Railway's entire stock at that time is seen, including Class 30 'Little Giant' 4-4-2 SANSPAREIL and seven Bassett-Lowke four wheeled open coaches, all shipped back from NGR's Oslo Exhibition Railway, plus three open wagons, a coach and a brakevan purchased from Sir Arthur Heywood at Duffield Bank. At this time the Railway had only been opened to Eskdale Green and a disconnected 3'0" gauge siding from the earlier railway survives in the foreground.
(74) The Heywood locomotives are very rarely featured on contemporary postcards, publishers evidently considering the scale model engines more attractive.However in the early 1960's the Ravenglass and Eskdale RPS published a 'historical' series of RP cards which include Heywood 0-6-OT ELLA preparing to leave Ravenglass on a Bank Holiday in 1923 with a relief train consisting of some of the four wheel hopper wagons, supplied by Francis Theakston Ltd. of Crewe for carriage of granite, hastily converted to passenger stock for the day.

(75) The well known photographers Sankey's of Barrow-in-Furness naturally included some cards of the reconstructed Ravenglass and Eskdale Railway in their range. This view taken circa 1915-16 shows SANS PAREIL and three Bassett-Lowke four wheel coaches posed near Muncaster Mill. The 'overscale' size of the original 3'0" gauge line's 30 lb/yd rails which have simply been regauged to 15" on the original sleepers can be contrasted with the 'scale' 7½ lb rail on which JOHN ANTHONY is standing in the picture below.   (76) LPC produced a beautiful colour printed set of six cards of the Ravenglass and Eskdale but once again used one photograph not taken in Cumberland. This picture was taken at Captain J.E.P. Howey's home Staughton Manor and shows Howey posing with JOHN ANTHONY, specially renamed GIGANTIC for this occasion, although when sold to the Eskdale line in 1916 it was renamed again to COLOSSUS – causing untold confusion to future historians! Howey did not revive the Staughton Manor Railway on his return from a German POW camp, but after failing to buy the Eskdale line went on to greater things on Romney Marsh.

Four cards featuring the Romney, Hythe and Dymchurch Railway, whose management were commendably alert to the publicity value of postcards.   (77) The Railway opened in 1926 and the first locomotives were two cylinder 4-6-2's based on the LNER A1 Pacifics. Needing more powerful locomotives, the Railway's owner, Captain J.E.P. Howey, commissioned two three cylinder versions, named TYPHOON and HURRICANE. Howey had good contacts with the LNER through his friendship with FLYING SCOTSMAN's designer Nigel Gresley, and was able to obtain this publicity shot of TYPHOON alongside her full size 'prototype' at Kings Cross shed in May 1927. This was published as No. 22 in a series of cards produced for the RH & DR by F. Moores.   (78) Between 1927 and 1931 passenger traffic was worked by the Pacifics and two 4-8-2's, one of these, HERCULES (as she ran for a short period in the late 'twenties without nameplates) is seen at Dymchurch, which in the early days was the terminal point of some short distance workings. The caption to this card (one of a series of 12) reads 'train arriving at Dymchurch' though in fact the stance of the train crew clearly shows that HERCULES is being coupled up prior to departure!

TRAIN ARRIVING DYMCHURCH STATION. ROMNEY, HYTHE AND DYMCHURCH RAILWAY. No. 6.

HYTHE. MINIATURE RLY.　　　　　　　　　　　　　　　　　　　　　　　　　　　　　　B963

While New Romney was the 'Headquarters' of the RH & DR, for the majority of passengers their first sight of the Railway was at Hythe. These two cards illustrate the rapid development of Hythe station as it was adapted to cope with the onslaught of passengers.　　(79) A Photochrom card showing the station before 1930 with its original short overall roof and the single storey Light Railway Restaurant (centre left). A Pacific, probably SOUTHERN MAID, with a train of semi-open four-wheelers, awaits departure for New Romney while a 4-8-2 shunts empty stock on the right.　　(80) is a 1934/35 view with the station roof greatly extended and the Restaurant having grown to two storeys. NORTHERN CHIEF departs with a train of new saloon coaches, built from 1934 onwards by Robert Hudsons and the Hythe Cabinet and Joinery Works. Providing a hitherto unmatched standard of comfort on the 15″ gauge, these were considered 'newsworthy' enough to be the subject of a postcard. One of the Canadian outline Pacifics is just visible on the right.

WORLD'S SMALLEST RAILWAY NEW SALOON COACHES AT HYTHE STATION　　　　　　　　　42A

Miniature Railway, Fairbourne.

Another long-lived miniature line is the Fairbourne Railway. Converted to 15″ gauge from a derelict 2′0″ gauge horse tramway by Narrow Gauge Railways Ltd. in 1916 it has been the subject of numerous postcards. These two cards are both from the period between the wars when the line was run very much on a shoestring by a local property company.   (81) Something seems to be amiss with COUNT LOUIS (the sole motive power at this time) and staff and passengers wait anxiously while the youthful driver examines his engine. Due to the exposed nature of the line, the prevailing wind which whipped sand into bearings and axleboxes was a constant problem, resulting in high maintenance bills and occasional engine failures. Also visible in this view are Friog Slate Quarries (centre, above Hotel).   (82) This Photochrom 'Celesque' series card was probably published in the 1920's and shows COUNT LOUIS with the Railway's entire stock at the beach terminus. Barmouth railway bridge can be glimpsed in the background. Following a period of closure and dereliction in World War 2, the line was revived by a group of Midlands businessmen in 1946.

FAIRBOURNE. MINIATURE RAILWAY.

50859

83

(83) The Fairbourne's new owners completely rebuilt the line, adding new stock and locomotives, including a pair of 2-4-2 tender locos KATIE and SIAN, of Great Western appearance but 'narrow gauge' rather than 'miniature' proportions. Both were built by the G. & S. Engineering Co. to the design of E.W. Twining in 1959 and 1963 respectively. Even this relatively modern J. Arthur Dixon card of SIAN leaving Fairbourne is now history, however, as the Railway has recently changed hands and has been completely rebuilt as a 12¼" gauge line of very different appearance.   (84) Opened in August 1948, the ¾ mile long line at Valley Gardens, Saltburn, North Yorkshire was originally worked by the pioneer Bassett Lowke petrol locomotive from Blakesley Hall (see (69) now named ELIZABETH. Around 1960 this was joined by PRINCE CHARLES, one of Mr. Barlow's 4-6-2 diesel electrics from Southport which is shown here in this sepia card, still running in its original livery. The 'smoke and steam' seen gushing from the chimney has been faked in during the printing process.

84

White City Station, Llewelyns Miniature Railway, Southport

85

The miniature railway at Southport is now the oldest surviving 15″ gauge railway in Britain and its history is well recorded in numerous postcards. Opened in 1911 by Mr. G.V. Llewelyn, a local postman and engineered by Henry Greenly, for the first five years of its life an official postcard was published each year showing a Bassett-Lowke "Little Giant" Atlantic and train posed in exactly the same spot in the station, the year being specially painted on the locomotive's front buffer beam for the photograph. (85) is the final (1915) one of the five cards, an island platform having been built since the previous year's card. The 1911 card showed the original Class 10 'Little Giant' PRINCE OF WALES, all the others (as here) show its more powerful successor, Class 20 KING GEORGE V. (86) Photochrom 'Celesque' series 53288 shows the same scene about 1921, by which time a single wide platform had replaced the pair of platforms of 1915, and much other improvement work has been undertaken. Sadly, by contrast with the upper view, passengers seem scarce.

SOUTHPORT MINIATURE RAILWAY

86

87

Brothers under the skin . . . . Despite their vastly different outward appearance, both locomotives shown on this page are mechanically identical 4-6-2 diesel-electric locomotives built by Mr. H.N. Barlow of Southport. (87) In the post-War period Mr. Barlow was a prolific builder of miniature railway equipment and designed a sturdy diesel electric 'steam outline' loco loosely based on a Gresley A4. DUKE OF EDINBURGH was one of these, being built in 1948 for the Lakeside Miniature Railway at Southport which Mr. Barlow had taken over.   (88) The delightful cartoons of Rowland Emmett with their numerous mechanical absurdities enlivened the pages of 'Punch' in the austere 1940's so for the 1951 Festival of Britain Emmett's 'Far Twittering and Oyster Creek Railway' (with a slight change of name from 'Twittering' to 'Tottering') was brought to life by Mr. Barlow as a 15" gauge railway in Battersea Park. All three Battersea locomotives utilised Barlow's standard chassis, No. 1 NELLIE being a 'conventional' saddletank, No. 2 NEPTUNE an interesting marriage of paddlesteamer and locomotive, whilst No. 3 WILD GOOSE appeared to be a hot air balloon on rails. All three locomotives were illustrated on Valentine's cards which despite their relative modernity are highly sought after today.

MODELS, RAILWAYS AND LOCOMOTIVES

Geo. E. Flooks' Miniature Railway, "Woodside," Bricket Wood, near St. Alban's.

Around the turn of the Century successful 'model' railways capable of carrying passengers began to be developed commercially. An early example was the 10¼" gauge line at Bricket Wood built by Fred Smithies and George Flooks, worked originally by an 0-4-4T NIPPER built by Flooks from a design by Henry Greenly. Published sources claim this line closed in 1904 following an accident to Flooks, however this card which was posted in St Albans on August 4th 1905 with the message "we all went to Bricket Wood last Saturday and went on this railway" conclusively proves that to be incorrect. The locomotive remains unidentified. (90) For a while in the 1930's the 9½" gauge was much in vogue for both private and commercial miniature railways. Stock was built to a scale of two inches to the foot, and Bassett-Lowkes supplied a standard Atlantic 4-4-2 based on a G.N.R. prototype. One of these operated the Southsea (Hants) Miniature Railway, this late 1930's view shows the train arriving back at the terminus. Note the elegant rolling stock, and staff in full railway uniform. The line was regauged to 10¼" after the War, and still operates today.

BACK AGAIN.   Southsea Miniature Railway.

WHARFEDALE MINIATURE RAILWAY

(91) Despite its impressive appearance this Atlantic loco is only 5 inch gauge! The Wharfedale Miniature Railway operated in the 1930's and 40's as an adjunct to a caravan saleroom at Ben Rhydding, near Ilkley in Yorkshire. BEN RHYDDING was built in Leeds in 1940/41 by a Mr. Leach and was one of two locos, the other being a 2-6-4T loosely based on a County Donegal prototype. (92) In its day the Farnborough Miniature Railway, near Camberley, Surrey, was the most extensive 10¼" gauge line in the country. Opened in 1935, by 1938 it was three miles long, had been renamed the Surrey Border & Camberley Railway, and worked an intensive service 12 hours a day. Six of the eight locomotives were GWR style machines built by H.C.S. Bullock, the other two were 2¼ ton 2-6-6-2 Beyer Garratts built by Kitson's of Leeds in 1938. This view shows the impressive Farnborough Green terminus. The line closed at the outset of War in 1939 but much of the stock and the locomotives subsequently found new homes, one as far away as New Delhi.

THE FARNBOROUGH (HANTS) MINIATURE RAILWAY

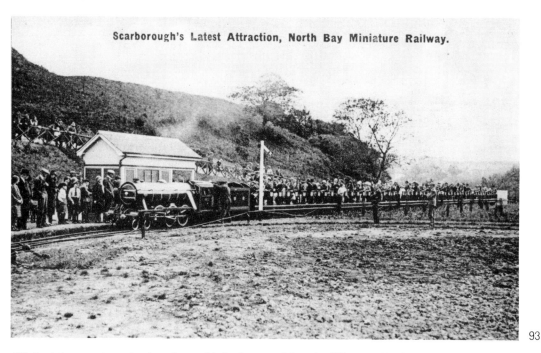

Scarborough's Latest Attraction, North Bay Miniature Railway.

(93) A miniature railway that has changed little during its life is the 20" gauge North Bay Railway opened at Scarborough in 1931. This early card by local Publishers E.T.W. Dennis & Sons shows one of the two very fine steam outline diesel locomotives built by Hudswell Clarke as scale models of an LNER A3 Pacific. Both are still in service today. In the depressed 1930's Hudwells built a number of similar miniature locomotives for Blackpool, Leeds, Morecambe and Butlins, when order for commercial locomotives were scarce.   (94) Typical of the post War miniature railway was the 10¼" gauge line at Colwyn Bay in North Wales. About 550 yards long it was opened by the local Council who sold out to a Mr. Spilstead about 1952. Sole motive power was PRINCE CHARLES, a 4-6-0 loosely based on the LMS Black Five and built by Carland Engineering. This firm built several 10¼" and 15" engines to this same general design in the late 1940's. PRINCE CHARLES was sold for preservation in 1971, being replaced by a home built 'Hymek' style Bo-Bo diesel. This is another nice card by Valentine's of Dundee, whose coverage of obscure miniature lines was commendably thorough.

MINIATURE RAILWAY. COLWYN BAY

W.6127

(95) Kerr's Miniature Railway, Arbroath, celebrated its 50th anniversary in 1985, having started as a 7¼" gauge line in 1935. It was converted to 10¼" gauge in 1938 and has used a variety of motive power, both steam and i.c. This 1948 view shows the Arbroath terminus with a Bullock 4-6-2 SILVER JUBILEE (right) and a petrol driven Atlantic on the turntable, and was produced as a Valentine's card.   (96) We end with a 'puzzle picture'. Miniature railways are much less common in Europe than in the UK, and it comes as a great surprise to find an example in Portugal. The location of the line is unknown, but the gauge appears to be about 10¼", and the locomotive a 4-6-0 of typically French design. The caption translates 'Humanitarian Association of Volunteer Firemen'. Even the publishers of this card are anonymous, but their endeavours have ensured that this attractive little line, and its young passengers, will take their place in history.

APPENDIX 1 – The Railways

Card No.	Railway	Gauge	Main route	Opened	Closed
1	Penmaenmawr Granite Quarry	3'0"	Internal	c 1870	1967
2,5,6	Festiniog	1'11½"	Portmadoc – Blaenau Festiniog	1836	1946-54
3	Penrhyn	1'10¾"	Port Penrhyn – Bethesda	1801	1962
4	Dinorwic Quarry	1'10¾"	Internal	1870	1969
5	Welsh Highland	1'11½"	Portmadoc (New) – Dinas Jcn.	1923	1937
7	North Wales Narrow Gauge	1'11½"	Dinas Jcn. – Rhydd-ddu	1877	1916
8-10	Talyllyn	2'3"	Towyn (Wharf) – Abergynolwyn	1865	N/A
11	Glyn Valley Tramway	2'4½"	Chirk – Glynceiriog	1873	1935
12	Corris	2'3"	Machynlleth – Aberllefeni	1883	1948
13, 14	Welshpool and Llanfair	2'6"	Welshpool – Llanfair Caerinion	1903	1956-63
15	Southwold	3'0"	Halesworth – Southwold	1879	1929
16	Campbeltown and Macrihanish	2'3"	Campbeltown – Macrihanish	1877	1932
17, 18	Leek and Manifold Valley	2'6"	Waterhouses – Hulme End	1904	1934
19-21	Lynton and Barnstaple	1'11½"	Barnstaple – Lynton	1898	1935
22	Ashover	1'11⅝"	Ashover (Butts) – Clay Cross	1925	1950
23(71)	Sand Hutton	1'3" 1'6"	Sand Hutton Estate Warthill – Claxton/Bossall	1912 1922	1920 1932
24	Rye and Camber Tramway	3'0"	Rye – Camber Sands	1895	1939
25, 26	Isle of Man Railways	3'0"	Douglas – Peel St. Johns – Ramsey Douglas – Port Erin	1873 1879 1874	1968 1968 N/A
27, 28	Manx Electric	3'0"	Douglas – Ramsey	1893	N/A
29	Groudle Glen	2'0"	Lhen Coan – Sea Lion Rocks	1896	1962
30	Jersey	3'6"	St. Helier – Corbiere	1870	1936
31, 32	Snowdon Mountain Tramroad (later Railway)	80 cm	Llanberis – Snowdon summit	1897	N/A
33, 34	Vale of Rheidol	1'11½"	Aberystwyth – Devils Bridge	1902	N/A
35	Volks Electric	2'9"	Palace Pier (Brighton) – Black Rock	1883	N/A
36	Hythe Pier	2'0"	Hythe Pier (Hants)	c 1921	N/A
37	Trentham Gardens	2'0"	Trentham Gdns, Stoke on Trent	1935	N/A
38	Drusillas Zoo	2'0"	Drusillas Zoo & Tea Gardens, Berwick (Sussex)	1947	N/A
41	Snailbeach District	2'4"	Pontesbury – Snailbeach	1877	1946
43	Cork and Muskerry	3'0"	Cork – Blarney/Donoughmore Coachford	1887	1934
44	Cavan and Leitrim	3'0"	Belturbet – Arigna/Dromod	1887	1959
45-47	Clogher Valley	3'0"	Tynan – Maguiresbridge	1887	1941
48	County Donegal Railways Joint Committee	3'0"	Strabane – Londonderry/Letterkenny/ Glenties/Killybegs/Ballyshannon	1862-1905	1954- (D'ry) 1947 (Gl's) 1959 (rest)

APPENDIX 1 – The Railways (Cont.)

Card No.	Railway	Gauge	Main route	Opened	Closed
51-53	Woolwich Arsenal	1'6"	Internal	1871	c1964
55	CF de Puy de Dome	metre	Clermont Ferrand (Pl Lamastre) Puy de Dome (Sommet)	1907	1926
56	Rotterdamshe Tramweg Maatschappij	metre	Rotterdam – Oostvoorne/ Hellevoetsluis	1898	1965
57	Vitznau – Rigi Bahn	4'8½"	Vitznau – Rigi Kulm	1871	N/A
58	Elavador do Monte	metre	Funchal (Pombal) – Terreiro de Luta	1891	1942
59	Deutsche Reichbahn	75cm	Freital Hainsberg – Kurort Kipsdorf	—	N/A
60	Achenseebahn	metre	Jenbach – Achensee	1889	N/A
61	Matheran Steam Tramway	2'0"	Neral – Marathan	1902	N/A
62	Darjeeling Himalaya	2'0"	New Jalpaiguri/Siliguri Jcn. – Darjeeling	1880/ 1	N/A
63	Mount Washington cog	4'8"	Marshfield – Summit Station	1868/ 9	N/A
64	Victoria Mill, Queensland	2'0"	Internal	c1905	N/A
65	Khartoum Tram	2'0"	Khartoum – Omdurman North/ Shambat	1904	1949
66	CF Vicineaux du Mayumbe	610mm	Boma – Tchela	1898	N/A
67	Blackpool Miniature	1'3"	South Shore (circuit)	1905	1910
68	Rhyl Miniature	1'3"	Marine Lake (circuit)	1911	1985
69,70	Blakesley Hall	1'3"	Blakesley (SMJR) – Blakesley Hall	1903	1947
71-76	Ravenglass and Eskdale	3'0" 1'3"	Ravenglass – Boot Ravenglass – Dalegarth	1875 1915	1912 N/A
77-80	Romney, Hythe and Dymchurch	1'3"	Hythe – Dungeness	1926/ 27	N/A
81-83	Fairbourne	1'3"	Fairbourne – Barmouth Ferry	1916	N/A
84	Saltburn Miniature	1'3"	Valley Gardens – Cat Nab	1948	1973
85-86	Llewelyns Miniature, Southport	1'3" }	White City – Lake Side	1911	
87	Lakeside Miniature, Southport	1'3"			N/A
88	Far Tottering & Oyster Creek (later Festival Gardens Min. Rly.)	1'3"	Festival of Britain Pleasure Gardens & Funfair	1951	1972
89	Woodside Miniature	10¼"	Bricket Wood, Nr St. Albans	1904	—
90	Southsea Miniature	9½"	Southsea, Hants (seafront)	1932	N/A
91	Wharfedale Miniature	5"	Caracars, Ben Rhydding	1932	by 1971
92	Farnborough Miniature (later Surrey Border and Camberley)	10¼"	Farnborough Green – Camberley	1935	1939
93	Scarborough Miniature	1'8"	Peasholm Park – Scalby Mills	1931	N/A
94	Colwyn Bay Miniature	10¼"	Colwyn Bay (seafront)	1949	N/A
95	Kerrs, Arbroath	10¼"	West Links Park, Arbroath	1935	N/A

APPENDIX 2 – The Postcards

Card No.	Type	Publisher	Series, reference etc.	Date	Value
1	Tinted		Renshaw	c 1905	£3
2	Tinted	Valentine's	19660	c 1902	£3
3	Real photo B/W	Real Photographic (Broadstairs)		c 1955	75p
4	Real photo B/W	Maid Marian Locomotive Fund		1966	75p
5	Sepia	Photochrom	59830	1924	£3
6	Colour	J. Arthur Dixon	Wales 1140	1958	75p
7	Real photo B/W	F. Moores		c 1904	£1.50
8	Tinted	F. Frith & Co.	77789	PU1929	£3
9	Sepia	Talyllyn Railway	TR1	1951	£2
10	Sepia	Talyllyn Railway	TR3	1951	£1.50
11	Tinted		Perfection 1255	c 1905	£5
12	Real photo B/W	Brockham Museum Association	CRS/4	1939	£1
13	Sepia	F. Frith & Co.	WPL 35	c 1955	£1.50
14	Real photo B/W	Welshpool and Llanfair Rly.	Official	1964	£1
15	Real photo B/W	Photomatic Ltd.		c 1910	N
16	Tinted	(1)		c 1910	£8
17	Real photo B/W	R & R Bull, Ashbourne		1904	£4
18	Tinted	North Staffordshire Railway	Official	1904	£2
19	Tinted	F. Frith & Co.	59449	PU1913	£1.50
20	Real photo B/W	L & GRP		c 1930	£1.50
21	B/W	(2)		c 1930	£4
22	Real photo B/W	R. Sneath, Sheffield		c 1925	£4
23	Real photo B/W	Photomatic Ltd		1927	N
24	Tinted	(1)		c 1935	£3
25	Real photo B/W	Photomatic Ltd		1956	N
26	Real photo B/W	IOM Railway Assoc.	IMRA/1	1967	£1.50
27	B/W	Boots Cash Chemists	Pelham series No. 595	PU1906	£2
28	Tinted	(1)		PU1907	£2
29	Tinted	Valentine's	21794	1896	£8
30	B/W	Louis Levy	Jersey 119	1913	£2
31	Tinted	London & North Western Rly.	Official	1896	£1.50
32	Sepia	Valentine's		PU1909	£2
33	Tinted	Pictorial Stationery Co. Ltd.	Autochrom colour photo	PU1905	£3
34	Tinted	Photochrom	Celesque 39591	c 1905	£1.50
35	Sepia	(1)		c 1920	£5
36	Real photo B/W	Dearden and Wade	Sunny South Real Photo	c 1955	75p
37	Real photo B/W	Valentine's	K6273	c 1950	£2
38	Sepia	F. Frith & Co.	TS BWK 34	c 1950	£1.50
39	Sepia (3)	W.G. Bagnall Ltd.	E1906	1909	£2
40	Sepia (3)	W.G. Bagnall Ltd.	E2081	1918	£2
41	Sepia (3)	W.G. Bagnall Ltd.	E1797	1906	£2

Card No.	Type	Publisher	Series, reference etc.	Date	Value
42	Real photo B/W	Hudswell Clarke & Co. Ltd.		1946	£2
43	B/W	Loco Publishing Co.	324	1905	£8
44	Tinted	(1)	Gems of Irish Transport series 1	c 1955	£1
45	Real photo B/W	L & GRP	7152	1933	£1.50
46	Real photo B/W	L & GRP	N – 1724	1933	£1.50
47	Real photo B/W	L & GRP	7158	1933	£1.50
48	Tinted		Gems of Irish Transport series 1	c 1955	£1
49	Real photo B/W	(1)		c 1917	£2
50	Tinted	unknown (France)		c 1905	£4
51	Real photo B/W	Brockham Museum Assoc.	RAR/1	1921	£2
52	Real photo B/W	Brockham Museum Assoc.	RAR/8	1921	£2
53	Real photo B/W	Brockham Museum Assoc.	RAR/6	1921	£2
54	Real photo B/W	(1)	No. 3	1918	£4
55	B/W	Neurdein & Cie, Paris	214	c 1910	£2
56	Real photo B/W	Uitgave Firma W van der Linden	B-75	1965	£1
57	Tinted	Vitznau-Rigi-Bahn	Serie 47 Officielle Ansichkarte No. 2	PU1907	£2
58	Tinted	Unknown (Madeira)	BP No. 101	c 1905	£1
59	Real photo B/W	Reichenbach (Vogtl)		c 1980	N
60	Colour	Foto Werniger, Jenbach		c 1970	N
61	Tinted	unknown (India)	184183	c 1910	£3
62	Tinted	Macropolo & Co., Calcutta	D436	c 1905	£3
63	Tinted	American Post Card Co. Boston	3A63	c 1925	£2
64	Colour	Peer Productions	PH51-4935/55-7266	c 1970	75p
65	Sepia	Gordon Stationery & Bookstores, Khartoum	No 42	c 1910	£2
66	B/W	Unknown (Belgium)		PU1920	£1.50
67	B/W	Miniature Railways of Great Britain		1905	£2.50
68	Sepia	Bassett-Lowke Ltd		PU1911	£2
69	Tinted	Loco Publishing Co.		1914	£2.50
70	Real photo B/W	Lens of Sutton		1914	N
71	B/W	Bassett-Lowke Ltd.		1913	£3
72	Sepia	W.J. Bassett-Lowke		1914	£3
73	Sepia	Meckin's Real Photo		1915	£2
74	Real photo B/W	Ravenglass & Eskdale Railway Co.	Historical series No. 2	1923	75p
75	Real photo B/W	Sankey Photo Press Barrow	5575	1915/16	£2
76	Tinted	Loco Publishing Co.		1914	£3

APPENDIX 2 – The Postcards (Cont.)

Card No.	Type	Publisher	Series, reference etc.	Date	Value
77	Tinted	F. Moores For the R.H. & D.R.	Romney Hythe & Dymchurch Railway No. 22 (4)	1927	£1.50
78	Tinted	(1)	Romney Hythe & Dymchurch Railway No. 6 (4)	c 1930	£1.50
79	Tinted	Photochrom	B 9638	c 1928	£1.50
80	Tinted	(1)	World's Smallest Public Railway No. 12A	PU1936	£1.50
81	Sepia	(1)		c 1932	£2
82	Tinted	Photochrom	Celesque 50859	c 1925	£3
83	Colour	J. Arthur Dixon	Natural colour photogravure SP 1377	1964	75p
84	Sepia	(1)	Pickering 22	c 1960	£1.50
85	Sepia	Llewellyn's Miniature Railway Ltd.	Official	1915	£2
86	Tinted	Photochrom	Celesque 53288	PU1923	£1.50
87	Real photo B/W	Lakeside Miniature Rly.		1957	£1
88	Real photo B/W	Valentine's (for Festival of Britain)	EV 32	1951	£3
89	Real photo B/W	W. Nicholls		PU1905	£3
90	Sepia	(1)		c 1935	£1.50
91	Sepia	(1)		c 1950	£1.50
92	Real photo B/W	Farnborough Miniature Rly.	Official	c 1936	£.150
93	B/W	E.T.W. Dennis & Sons	32	1931	£1
94	Sepia	Valentine's	Phototype W 6127	c 1955	£1.50
95	Sepia	Valentine's	Phototype B5095	PU1954	£1
96	B/W	Unknown (Portugal)		c 1920	£1

Notes

Value: Values are at 1.1.86 level, assume the card is in mint condition, and should be read as a comparative (rather than absolute) guide. N indicates nominal value.

Type: All cards are produced by a printing process, unless indicated 'Real photo'.

Date: Postally used date (PU) where available is quoted as being the most accurate guide to the age of a postcard. Other dates quoted are those on which the original photo was taken: publication date would normally be contemporaneous (for known variations see appropriate caption).

(1) No publisher name shown

(2) Original publisher unknown: republished by Lens of Sutton RP B/W: 'Value' in this case is estimated value of original card.

(3) Advertising card with technical data printed on reverse.

(4) Not the same series.

SELECTIVE BIBLIOGRAPHY

Narrow Gauge Album   P.B. Whitehouse   Ian Allan 1957
On the Narrow Gauge   P.B. Whitehouse   Nelson 1964
Narrow Gauge Railways of Europe   P.B. Whitehouse/J.B. Snell Ian Allan 1959
The English Narrow Gauge Railway   J.D.C.A. Prideaux   David & Charles 1976
The Welsh Narrow Gauge Railway   J.D.C.A. Prideaux   David & Charles 1976

Individual Railway Histories

Narrow Gauge Railways of Mid Wales   J.I.C. Boyd   Oakwood Press 1964
Railway Adventure   L.T.C. Rolt   Constable 1953
The Southwold Railway   A.R. Taylor/E.S. Tonks   Ian Allan 1979
The Ashover Light Railway   K.P. Plant   Oakwood Press
The Lynton & Barnstaple Railway   G.A. Brown/J.D.C.A. Prideaux/H.G. Radcliffe
    David & Charles 1964
The Isle of Man Railway   J.I.C. Boyd   Oakwood Press 1962
The Campbeltown & Macrihanish Light Railway   N.S.C. Macmillan   David & Charles 1970
The Ravenglass and Eskdale Railway   W.J.K. Davies   David & Charles 1968
The Romney, Hythe and Dymchurch Railway   W.J.K. Davies   David & Charles 1975
The Sand Hutton Light Railway   K.E. Hartley   Narrow Gauge Rly Society 1982
The Rye & Camber Tramway   P.A. Harding   P.A. Harding 1985

Miniature and Fifteen Inch Gauge Railways

Minimum Gauge Railways   Sir Arthur Heywood   Turntable Publications 1974
Miniature Railways Past and Present   A.J. Lambert   David & Charles 1982
Miniature Railways Volume 1 15" Gauge H. Clayton/M. Jacot/R. Butterell   Oakwood Press
The Duffield Bank and Eaton Hall Railways   H. Clayton   Oakwood Press
The Miniature World of Henry Greenly   E.A. Steel/E.H. Steel M.A.P. 1973
Miniature Railways Stockbook   R.H. Leithead   Narrotrack Ltd 1975

Postcards

The Picture Postcard and its Origins   Frank Staff   Lutterworth 1979
Picture Postcards of the Golden Age   Tony and Valmai Holt   Postcard Publishing Co. 1978
Picture Postcards and their Publishers   Tony Byatt   Golden Age Postcards 1978
Collecting   Postcards 1894-1914   W. Duval/V. Monahan   Blandford Press 1978
Collecting Postcards 1914-1930   V. Monahan   Blandford Press 1980
Picture Postcard Annual   Brian & Mary Lund   Reflections of a Bygone Age 1980-86

Railways and Postcards

Railways in Britain on Old Picture Postcards   Brian Lund   Reflections of a Bygone Age 1983
Edwardian Postcards of Road and Rail Transport   D.E. Brewster   Oakwood Press 1982
Official Railway Postcards of the British Isles Vol 1 LNWR
                                                 Vol 2 GWR   R. Silvester   BPH Publications

Periodicals

Picture Postcard Monthly (monthly) –   Reflections of a Bygone Age, 15 Debdale Lane, Keyworth, Nottingham, NG12 5HT

The Narrow Gauge (quarterly)   Narrow Gauge Railway Society, c/o Peter Slater, Hole in the
Narrow Gauge News (bi monthly)   Wall, Bradley, Ashbourne, Derbyshire.